Rocket Reading International

Presents

Rocket Writing

By

Carol Anne Campodonica

Copyright 2024,2023,2022

No form of the material may be electronically or mechanically copied, stored in a computer, flash drive, SD Card, camera, I-Phone, Facebook, Facetime, the internet or any other technological devices.

Rocket Reading International reserves the right to revise and improve informational pages as it sees fit without notification.

Title and First Paragraph

Some people are verbal, and others write their words and thoughts on paper. In my schooling, there were assignments that delt with writing. However, many of the instructors were not taught how to present writing. They knew how to write, but they lacked the skill of teaching writing. Composition books, spend time on teaching the different parts of English Grammar. Instead, they neglected giving the necessary skills as a beginner or non-writer could use.

It is my desire in Rocket Writing to show the techniques that help writing to be successful for students of all ages. A *prepositional phrase* should be written in front of a simple sentence. A list of prepositional words are included and should be memorized. Select a *prepositional word* to make *a phrase*. That prepositional phrase will be written in front of a simple sentence. Be sure to place a comma after the phrase and before a *simple sentence*.

Before writing begins on an essay, you need to *practice* writing *a compound sentence.* Two simple sentences joined by a conjunction make a compound sentence. At least one compound sentence should be written in each paragraph. A compound sentence helps the flow of words within a paragraph.

A transition word seems to be a well-kept secret and is often used in writing.

Every transitional word must be written before a simple sentence. Be sure to include the comma after the transition word and before a simple sentence.

Prepositional words and *transitional* words help a sentence or paragraph from being boring. You should introduce a *fact,* or an *example* in a paragraph. A compound sentence or simple sentences may be used to *support* the *title* of the article. By giving a reasonable answer as to why you chose a particular example to share, you will give a boost to your style of writing. Transitional words or phrases help to connect an example and it also connects paragraphs. A Transitional phrase is written almost at the end of a paragraph, or it may be the last sentence in a paragraph.

Beginners should practice writing an introduction listing three nouns in a series by placing a comma after every noun. As writing advances, students will write a complete sentence or two for each noun mentioned. The subject of a simple sentence for beginners will be a friend's name, or a person's name. A pronoun may be used to start a simple sentence. In addition, the name of a town or park may begin a sentence. Some simple sentences may begin with an object like a table or vase.

In Rocket Writing students should select a title they have a lot of knowledgeable information about, the title they chose. In addition, it is easier to find research material for writing. By students selecting three different nouns that are applicable to the subject, those three different nouns will become the introduction to each of the three paragraphs that they will write about. In fact, students should be reminded of the order of nouns listed, is important to keep the sequential order of nouns in writing.

1. All writing must have a **title**.

2. Your *first* paragraph is called the **Introduction**.

3. Your first sentence will give the reader some information about the title.

4. Before writing, select *three* **nouns** that relate to the title.
    Example-Title: **Winter Clothes** = sweater, jacket, and dress suit.

5. In some cases, three different ***adjectives*** must describe a noun. An **introduction** is the first sentence of a paragraph. Prepositional phrases are underlined once. It is best to find nouns to use in the introduction paragraph. Title: **ice cream**. (Three nouns: ***strawberry*** ice cream, ***vanilla*** ice cream, and ***chocolate*** ice cream).

6. The **second** paragraph will use the *first* noun mentioned in the introduction. Within the paragraph, a *compound* sentence is needed along with a few *simple sentences*. Also, included in the paragraph are *facts* and *examples* that support the title. Please don't forget to write a prepositional phrase with a

simple sentence and include a transitional phrase before a simple sentence near the end of the paragraph.

7. If possible, the **third** paragraph should begin with a *prepositional phrase*. If a second prepositional phrase is included in the third paragraph, your writing will be stronger. Include a compound sentence and several simple sentences. A reasonable explanation for writing the *facts* and introducing *examples* to support the introduction and title. Again, a transitional word or transitional phrase near the end of the paragraph is needed to connect both paragraphs.

8. Subsequently, the **fourth** paragraph should begin with a prepositional phrase. Some simple sentences and one or two compound sentences that support the title. Include a transitional phrase to tie or connect the fourth sentence with the conclusion paragraph. Consequently, do not forget to support your writing with a fact and an example or two.

9. The **fifth** paragraph is a *conclusion*, or *summary* about the title and the main points of your introduction. A Thesaurus is needed to replace the nouns that were chosen in the introduction to introduce the different paragraphs. No writing was provided in the conclusion, or summary area.

10. Prepositional phrases and transitional phrases used by writers are underlined. A comma is placed after the prepositional

phrase and the transitional phrase when a noun or subject is present in a simple sentence. As a reminder, the name of a *person*, *pronoun*, or *object* like a vase or *town* may be used to begin a simple sentence.

11. Every time you read a *newspaper*, *magazine* or a *story*, **observe** the *preposition* in the article. Notice how the prepositional phrase helps a simple sentence flow smoothly.

12. **Examine** carefully how a *transitional word* **connects** a paragraph with another paragraph. Observe how the last sentence of a paragraph helps to reveal the subject of the following paragraph. A transitional phrase may connect ideas within a paragraph too.

13. Some of the stories show how to use prepositional words beyond a phrase and they are underlined. A prepositional phrase has no verb and will be underlined once.

14. Transitional phrases may have a verb within its phrase, and the sentence will be underlined *twice*. A transitional phrase will begin a sentence.

15. Some stories may begin with a question, instead of a prepositional phrase. It is okay to begin writing with a question in the introduction.

16. Select a topic you have experienced or know a lot of information about it. It will be easier to find the following: facts, examples, and an experience to share when reading to your classmates. Do not forget to include the punctuation marks when reading your article to the class. Others will learn and appreciate the time you take to read and include the punctuation marks.

17. Read the story about socks without the prepositional words and transitive words, and you will notice the difference it makes when a prepositional word and phrase have been added to the writing. Transitive words smooth out the wrinkles and the sentences are easily read because it helps connect sentences and paragraphs.

18. The fifth paragraph has no summary. The summary can be written in class. Students should replace the noun words in the introduction. A list of summary words has been provided. Prepositions and transitive words will help connect ideas and will help to conclude with a strong ending for a writer.

19. The mini-lesson and examples shown will help create a quick and memorable knowledge on the comma, quotation marks, addressing a person, the word "or," comma in a series, comma in dates, semi-colons, colons, hyphens, parenthesis, brackets, and ellipses.

20. Rocket Writer touches on contractions, pronouns, adjectives that fall into three categories, helping verbs and action verbs. Examples are shown in each area.

21. For those who love to write a narrative or fictional story, many suggestions have been made about a major or minor character and how they relate to one another in the story.

22. Always indent each new paragraph.

23. Words of encouragement to help build the confidence of a student learning to write and punctuate properly: *fantastic, marvelous, fabulous, splendid, terrific, superb, brilliant, outstanding, good, very good, superior, and excellent*

24. Prepositional words are listed to enable the writer to use words in a sentence or paragraph. After the mini lesson, prepositional and transitional words become engaged with a simple sentence to illustrate the purpose of using the words listed in Rocket Writing.

Prepositions

about	above	across	after
against	along	among	around
at	before	behind	below
beneath	beside	between	beyond
but	by	considering	despite

down	during	except	for
from	in	inside	into
like	of	off	on
onto	out	outside	over
past	since	through	throughout
to	toward	under	underneath
until	up	upon	with
within	without		

Story #1
Title: *Socks*
(one paragraph)

(First, read <u>Socks</u> *once* with prepositions and transitional words and phrases and then *omit* the preposition and transitional words.)
And, you will see your writing will improve with the prepositions and transition words.

<u>**In**</u> *the morning*, I purchased a pair of socks and the socks disappeared. Last week I took the clothes out of the washing machine, and I had no socks. <u>***Again***</u>**,** I washed my clothes with my socks and only one sock was in the washing machine. <u>Meanwhile,</u> I placed a pair of socks in the washing machine, and I decided to keep a close eye on the washing machine. **<u>As</u>** *<u>a result,</u>* I found a boy and his girlfriend were sneaking in the laundry room and removing my socks. **<u>To</u>** *<u>sum up</u>*, I did not have to purchase a new washing machine.

* <u>Mini lessons are presented in punctuation after the story of "Socks".</u>*

Place a prepositional word or prepositional phrase in front of a simple sentence. Prepositions may have a noun in a prepositional phrase. (n = noun).
Sentences will follow to illustrate how to transform a simple sentence into a powerful sentence for the reader.

A comma is placed after a prepositional phrase and before the subject of a simple sentence. The subject of a simple sentence is a noun. A noun is a person (name), place, or thing. Also, pronouns can be the subject of a simple sentence.

         n
- <u>**In** the evening,</u> *I* walked to the store. (I = <u>*pronoun*</u> in the simple sentence).

         n
- <u>**Beneath** the fence,</u> the *snake* slithered across the grass (snake = <u>*animal*</u>).

         n
- <u>**Above** the clouds,</u> the *planes* flew overhead. (clouds = <u>*objects*</u>).

         n
- <u>**Along** the riverbank,</u> *Sam* saw fish swimming. (Sam = <u>*person*</u>).

         n
- <u>**After** lunch,</u> *we* ate dessert, (we = <u>*pronoun*</u>).

Transitive Words

Transitive words connect sentences and unite paragraphs. By using connectives, it helps to keep the thought process of the paragraph flowing smoothly. Some words may be on multiple lists.

The following list of words are transitional verbs, and they usually start a sentence.

and	again	besides	equally
equally important		finally	first
furthermore		important	in addition
lastly	more	moreover	nor
second			

- **Besides** working, *we* danced all night long. (we = *plural pronoun*).
- **Moreover,** *she* loves to golf with her friends. (she = *pronoun*).
- **Furthermore**, *Tom* will bring his boat to the lake. (Tom = *person*).
- **In addition, people** need to carefully examine programs and policies of candidates running for office. (people = *person*)
- **Again,** the *park* is a great place for a picnic. (park = *place*)

Connectives that can be used to add an idea to another idea- additions

again	also	and	and then
besides	finally	first	further
furthermore		in addition	last
moreover	next	in the first place	
second	still	too	

- **Moreover,** *we* will get together after work. (we = *plural pronoun*)
- **In** the first place, *she* is my sister. (she = *pronoun*)
- **Further,** *Sharon* will supervise the teenagers. (Sharon = *person*)

Common Transitional Words that may be used to Connect Paragraphs

It helps the reader to follow the thought from one paragraph to another paragraph.

accordingly	for example	otherwise
also	for instance	similarly
another	furthermore	such
as a result	in fact	then
at last	likewise	therefore
at this time	moreover	thus
consequently	nevertheless	too
finally	on the other hand	

To Show Contrast

although	and	at the same time	on the- other hand
even though	despite that	even so	in contrast
instead	for all that	however	in spite of
on the contrary	nevertheless	regardless	though
	otherwise	notwithstanding	

- **However,** *we* are not going to the movies with you tonight.
- **On** the contrary, *I* disagree with Robert's opinion about the movie.
- **Instead** of working, *Gabby* and *I* are going shopping.

To Show Results an Effect or Consequence

as a result	for	consequently
accordingly	hence	thus
therefore	outcome	in that case
because the	there upon	forthwith
aftermath	henceforth	up shot
matter of course	under those circumstances	

- **Consequently,** *George* lost his job at the bakery. (George = *person*)
- **In** that case, *Sandy* will have to pay for the parking ticket. (Sandy = *person*)

Explanatory Writing that Introduces Examples as Support

in other words	notably	in fact
to put it differently	including	in general
for one thing	like	in
particular	as an illustration	to be sure
in detail	in this case	namely
for example	for this reason	chiefly
besides	for instance	to put it-
another way	truly	indeed
to demonstrate	that is to say	certainly
to emphasize	with attention to	to repeat
by all means	surely	to clarify
markedly	to explain	another
to enumerate	such as	key point
important to realize	especially	specifically
first thing to remember	expressively	must be
most compelling evidence	surprisingly	frequently
remembered	significantly	
to point out	often overlooked	
with this in mind	on the positive side	
on the negative side		

- **By all means**, *we* need to support the football team.
- **Surprisingly,** the men saved the woman from drowning when her boat capsized.

Argumentative or Persuasive Writing to Express Opposition or an Alternative Idea
(popular words = italicized too)

accordingly	*for example*	*on the contrary*
again	*for instance*	*on the other hand*
although	*furthermore*	*otherwise*
another	hence	second
as a result	*if this be true*	such
at the same time	*in addition*	then too
besides	*in fact*	*therefore*
consequently	*in short*	thus
equally important	*moreover*	to sum up
finally	*nevertheless*	whereas
first	although this may be true	
but	in contrast	still
instead	different from	unlike
whereas	of course…	or
despite	yet	after all
conversely	in reality	otherwise
while	at the same time	albeit
however	in spite of	rather
be that as it may	regardless	then again
not with standing	above all	

- **On** the other hand, ***Timothy*** gave a positive speech *instead* of a negative speech for graduation.
- **In** reality, the *men* and *women* were disappointed with the high price of food.

Transitive Words to Express Agreement and Reinforce Ideas for the Reader

In the first place	**again**	**moreover**
as well as	**not only…**	**…but also**
to	**as a matter of fact**	
and	**together with**	**in like manner**
too	**of course**	**also**
in addition	**important**	**then**
likewise	**coupled with**	**equally**
comparatively	**in the same way**	**identically**
correspondingly	**first**	**second**
third	**uniquely**	**similarly**
not to mention	**as**	**additionally**
to say nothing of		

- **Likewise,** *everyone* is in agreement with Roger.
- **Naturally,** *we* are working to build another gym so everyone can exercise.

A Cause or Condition or Purpose that Includes a Specific Conditions or Intentions

in the event of	if	in case
granted	…then	provided that
as	so long as	unless
on (the) condition (that)	only	even if
for the purpose of	when	so that
with the intention	whenever	so as to
with this in mind	since	owing to

in the hope that	while	in as much as
for fear that	because of	due to
in order to	seeing	being that
in view of		

- **In** other words, *we* need to celebrate Veterans Day.
- **Since** working, *they* have decided to set aside time to offer better investment in the stock market.

Transitive Words that Envolve Time, Chronological Order and Sequence
(It can limit time, restrict time or define time)

at the present time	after	henceforth
from time to time	later	whenever
sooner or later	last	eventually
at the same time	until	meanwhile
up to the present time	since	further
to begin with	then	during
in due time	before	first
as soon as	hence	second
in the meantime	third	now
in a moment	when	in time
without delay	once	prior to
in the first place	about	forthwith
all of a sudden	next	
straightaway	at this instant	

- **Eventually**, *we* held our business meetings on Thursdays.

- **At the present time,** the *city* is experiencing a loss of electrical power.

Transitive Words that Deal with Space and Location

in the middle	here	further
to the left	to the right	there
beyond	in front of	next
nearby	on this side	down
where	wherever	in the distance
from	around	among
here and there	over	between
in the foreground	near	before
in the background	above	along side
in the center of	below	amid

- **In the distance,** *we* saw a star fall from space.
- **In the middle of the desert,** *they* found water.

Transitional Summary Words

all in all	altogether	as has been said
finally	in brief	in conclusion
in other words	in particular	in short
in simpler terms	in summary	on the whole
that is	therefore	to put it differently
to summarize	clearly	after all
to conclude	as has be noted	

- **Altogether,** the *women* will compete in sports.
- **All in all, we** will meet on July 4th next year to celebrate freedom in the U.S.A.

Transitional Words that are Action Words for a Resume

achieved	established	prepared	actively
evaluated	produced	administered	examined
programmed	executed	advanced	simplified
articulated	facilitated	qualified	assembled
finished	founded	refined	authorized
generated	reinforced	balanced	grew
revamped	began	held	broadened
clarified	improved	scheduled	managed
collaborated	coordinated	demonstrated	organized
participated	nurtured	supervised	

Transitional Words that are Self Descriptive Resume Words

accomplished	imaginative	realistic
active	incredible	reliable
adaptable	independent	resourceful
adept	integrity	respectful
aggressive	intelligent	responsible
ambitious	intense	result-driven
analytical	intuitive	results-oriented
articulate	inventive	self-reliant
artistic	knowledgeable	sense of humor
attentive	leader	sensible
	logical	skilled

Conjunctions

The joining of two simple *independent* clauses together by using a *Comma* and a *Conjunction*.

1. Jan goes to college, ***but*** Harry stays home.
2. The queen died from laughter, ***and*** we gave the queen a funeral.
3. Dad cooks, ***and*** Mom sets the table.
4. I will hold the ladder for you to come down, ***until*** I can climb the ladder.

Not All Conjunctions *Use* a Comma in a Sentence

1. Tom ***and*** Larry like to play baseball.
2. His mother ***and*** my mother are friends.
3. The boys cheered ***and*** clapped as the U.S. flag was raised on the football field.
4. Some girls from Russel School ***and*** George School played soccer.

Quotation Sentences

The first word in a quote is capitalized. A quotation mark is used to indicate a direct quote in a poem or words someone spoke, or brief words spoken in a speech. Never quote a whole speech.

asked	*inquired*	*demanded*
questioned	*remarked*	*responded*
exclaimed	*said*	

1. Jeff *asked*, "When do we eat?" (comma *before* quote)
2. "When do we eat?" *asked* Jeff. (question mark *after* quote—no comma)
3. Jill *remarked*, "You have beautiful dishes." (comma *before* quote)
4. "You have beautiful dishes," *remarked* Jill. (comma *after* quote)
5. Joe remarked, "We are ready to leave." (comma *before* quote)
6. "We are ready to leave," remarked Joe. (comma *after* quote)

Interrupted Quote

A quote that is interrupted by a person, the reader will find the *second half* of the quotation will have a lower-case letter and *not* a capital.

1. "Have you," Terry questioned, "***been*** working in the peaches this summer?"
2. "Where are the washed clothes," remarked Sue "***and*** the hand towels?"

Addressing a Person

In addressing a person a comma is placed *after* the name and *before* the name.

1. **Ellen**, I will bring you a new flowering plant for your patio.
2. We will split the money from the laundromat later, **William**.
3. Will you clean the windows for me, **Charlie**?

Word "OR"

In a sentence, a comma is used when two words are similar in meaning. A comma is placed before the word *"or"*.

1. Will the driving test be *simple*, **or** *easy*?
2. Ted bought a *bed,* **or** *cot* for his bedroom.
3. A *conclusion,* **or** *summary* is needed to end a story.

Comma in a Series

In a series of words, a comma separates each word in a sentence and a conjunction. A comma is needed between nouns, adjectives and verbs, etc.

1. It is time for Stan, Jeff, Nick, Charles, ***and*** Terry to clean the garage.

2. Rick ordered a pair of black pants, brown pants, two pairs of shorts, pajamas, shoes, ***and*** a jacket.
3. The bitter, tough, green, icy cold, lettuce, ***and*** cabbage were thrown away.

Comma in Dates

A comma separates the day from the year, and a comma separates the day of the week from the month.

1. We scheduled a business meeting on ***March*** 4, 2026.
2. On ***Friday***, May 1, 2028, I will buy a new car.
3. ***Monday,*** November 11, 2030 is Veteran Day.
4. ***29,*** June 2028, a garlic festival is planned in Gilroy.

Semi Colon

A semi colon is used between two independent sentences. A conjunction is *not* used when a semi colon is used. The first sentence shows a *comma* and *conjunction* connecting two independent sentences. A *semi colon* is used. The third sentence shows a transitive word is written after the semi colon, and a comma is used after the transitive word.

1. The queen got married***, and*** we honored the queen with a good luck party.
2. The queen got married***; we*** honored the queen with a good luck party.

3. The queen got married; ***therefore***, we honored the queen with a good luck party.

A. Henry goes to college***, but*** Susan stays home with the kids.
B. Henry goes to college***; Susan*** stays home with the kids.
C. Henry goes to college; ***however***, ***Susan*** stays home with the kids.

Colon

A colon is used at the end of a statement when a list of words are to be introduced. Words in a series are separated by a comma. First clause does not explain enough, and a colon is used for the second sentence to clarify the problem.

- In college, I signed up for several classes: algebra, geometry, English, history, and music.

- Peter purchased numerous camping items: a tent, ice chest, a barbeque grill, sleeping bags, paper plates, cups, and napkins.

- The mattress cover needs a double reinforced stitching to make the mattress cover useable: with latex, double sided stitching, and multiple rows.

A Variety of Colon Uses

- *In greeting of a business letter.*
    1. Dear Mr. Abbot:
    2. Dear Gentlemen:

- *Between the hour and minutes in time.*
    1. 10:00 A.M. meeting
    2. Party begins at 7:30 P.M.

- *Dividing the title from a subtitle*
    1. My Favorite Book: Gone with the Wind
    2. A Necessary Colon: Adopting Colon Writing

- *Name of chapter and verse in the Bible*
    1. John 3:16
    2. Romans 8:28

- *In naming a page number in a magazine*
    1. Newsweek 125: 68-78
    2. Time 101:21

- *Between the city and the publisher in bibliographical entry*
    1. California: Glencoe Publishing Co., Inc.
    2. New York: Harcourt, Brace & World, Inc.

Hyphen

Hyphenate numbers from *twenty-one to ninety-nine* when writing a letter or writing a check. Also, hyphenate fractions when they come before an adjective. Hyphenate a two - syllable word at the end of a sentence, when a small space is too limited to write the whole word.

1. thirty-four girls
2. two-thirds majority of students.

Hyphenate Compound Adjectives

There are two ways of writing a compound *adjective.* The most accurate is illustrated first.

1. A third-story room.   A room in the third story.
2. dark-colored glasses.   My glasses are a dark color.

Adjectives

An adjective will fall into one of the three categories. A word ending in "er" will compare two things. An adjective that ends in "est" will compare three or more things.

Positive (1)	Comparative (2)	Superlative (3)
old	older	oldest
far	farther	farthest
blue	bluer	bluest

Hyphenate Prefixes *before* Proper Nouns.

Use a hyphen before a proper noun like "ex-," "self,-" and the prefix "all."
Also, the prefix elect associated with nouns.

1. Pan-American
2. Pro-British
3. Anti-Russian
4. Governor elect

Use of a Dash

A dash shows a break in an important thought. A dash can be used after a first sentence is incomplete in clarity. The second sentence after the dash explains by clarifying the thought of the first sentence.

1. She forgot—the wedding vows—and the diamond bracelet.
2. The missing Trust papers—disappeared with the robbery.

Parentheses

Depending on the sentence, some _commas_ and _periods_ are placed _within_ parentheses, while it gives a small detail, that it is not important to the sentence.

- Congressman Dwarte (R., California) is Vice-Chair of the Subcommittee on Highways and Transit.
- She asked him, (a tasteless and tactless question) "Did you get fired?"

Brackets

Sometimes a sentence does not give enough information so, a bracket gives an explanation to the reader.

1. I am honored to be here [as leader] and to participate in a growing company.
2. The Republicans are always arguing (the party must reorganize) and we must [reorganize the Republican party] to win elections.

What to Underline?

Every title of a book must be underlined, all works of art (with pictures) musical compositions, including statues. Newspapers

and Magazines are underlined too. A broader view are ships, trains, and planes.

Books

- <u>Pride and Prejudice</u> or the <u>Adventures of Tom Sawyer</u>

Musicals

- <u>Peter and the Wolf</u> by Prokofiev or <u>Rhapsody in Blue</u> by Gershwin.

Famous Statues

- <u>Statue of Liberty</u> by Bartholdi.
- <u>Christ the Redeemer</u> by Paul Landowski.

Newspaper Names

- <u>Chicago Tribune</u> or the <u>Los Angeles Times</u>
- <u>Online Post</u>

Famous Ships

- <u>Titanic</u>
- <u>USS Arizona</u>

Famous Trains

- <u>Orient Express</u>
- <u>Glacier Express</u>

Famous Planes

- Wright Flyer
- Boeing 747-400

Ellipse

An ellipse in a sentence means few words have been omitted. The reader will have to make an assertion about what is missing or happened.

- The team stopped playing…a couple of team members got hurt.
- A large college club was started…but suddenly students began dropping out of the club.

Apostrophe

An apostrophe shows an omission of letters in a contraction word. *Never* use an apostrophe in a *personal* pronoun.

- Is my *Father's* hat sitting on the mantel?
- Barbara, it is a *man's* coat.

The s-sound that ends in a two-syllable word will have an apostrophe behind the word. Another "s" is not added to avoid confusion.

- Mrs. _Furness'_ car stopped working.
- The _princess'_ wedding will take place soon.
- The honeymoon couple will use _Odysseus'_ travel service.

A plural noun that does not end with an "s" will have an apostrophe and an "s" added to make a possessive noun.

1. We will attend the **_women's_** fashion show.
2. The **_children's_** games will begin at 10:00 A.M.

A plural noun ending in "s" will only add an apostrophe to make a possessive plural.

- The **_boys'_** gymnasium is packed with people who like basketball.
- We will play tennis on the **_Joneses'_** tennis court.

Words like minute, hour, day, week, month, year are illustrated below when they are used as a possessive adjective. Also, money requires an apostrophe when it is used as a possessive adjective.

- a minute's work
- a day's rest
- one cent's worth
- one dollar's worth

An apostrophe is added to plural letters, numbers, and signs.

- I have two 3's in mind.
- Please count the number of *and's* in a single paragraph.
- Did you know Mississippi is spelled with *four s's*, *four i's,* and two *p's?*

Contractions

Did you know a contraction is made up of two words? The word is combined together to make one word by omitting one or more letter's. Contraction are used in friendly letters, or referring to a quote that was said. However, documents must use both words in formal writing and not contractions.

I'm	=	I am
I'd	=	I would, I had
I'll	=	I will
I've	=	I have
you'll	=	you will
you'd	=	you would, you had
you've	=	you have
you're	=	you are
he'll	=	he will
he'd	=	he would, he had

he's	=	he is, he has
she'll	=	she will
she'd	=	she would, she had
she's	=	she is, she has
it'll	=	it will
it'd	=	it would, it had
it's	=	it is, it has
we've	=	we have
we'd	=	we would, we had
we'll	=	we will
we're	=	we are
they'll	=	they will
they'd	=	they would, they had
they've	=	they have
they're	=	they are
who's	=	who is, who has
who'd	=	who would, who had
that'll	=	that will
that'd	=	that would, that had
that's	=	that is, that has
let's	=	let us
aren't	=	are not

can't	=	cannot
couldn't	=	could not
didn't	=	did not
doesn't	=	does not
don't	=	do not
hadn't	=	had not
hasn't	=	has not
haven't	=	have not
isn't	=	is not
mustn't	=	must not
shouldn't	=	should not
wouldn't	=	would not
wasn't	=	was not
weren't	=	were not
won't	=	will not
there's	=	there is, there has
there'd	=	there would, there had
there'll	=	there will
there've	=	there have
what's	=	what is, what has
that's	=	that is, that has
who's	=	who is, who has
here's	=	here is, here has

Helping Verbs

A helping verb helps an action verb, but a helping verb can become a main verb.

am	**is**	**are**	**was**	**were**	**be**
been	**being**	**have**	**has**	**had**	**do**
does	**did**	**would**	**should**	**could**	**will**

Action Verbs

Some action verbs involve a mental thought process.

act	**dig**	**smile**	**break**	**fight**
teach	**fix**	**think**	**build**	**fly**
throw	**buy**	**give**	**thought**	

First Person Pronoun

	Singular	*Plural*
1st person	I	we
2nd	you	you
3rd	he/she/it	they

Possessive Pronouns

The following pronouns can become objects of verbs and prepositions.

my,   your,   his,   her,   its,   our,   their

Possessive Pronouns that Illustrate Ownership

mine,   our,   ours,   your,   yours,
his,   hers,   its,   their,   theirs,   whose

Singular

1st person	I	listen	listened
2nd person	you	listen	listened
3rd person	he/she	listens	listened

Plural

1st person	we	listen	listened
2nd person	you	listen	listened
3rd person	they	listen	listened

Descriptive Writing with Adjectives

The writer may use directions to help a character find a missing book that was stolen and is worth several thousand dollars. In addition, the writer will give a description of what the character sees, touches, hears, tastes and smells. Thus, the writer will keep the reader intrigued with the plot in the novel or short story.

above	beyond	on my left
across from	further	on my right
adjacent to	here	opposite
before me	near by	to the right
below	next to	

Also, using vivid directions helps the reader to visualize the characters emotional and complex issues according to the plot in the story.

- **In** the distance, *we* saw the sunset.   (we = *pronoun*)
- **On** my right**, Jason** sat with his son. (Jason = *person*)
- **Beyond** the ridge, the *fog* began to lift. (fog = *thing*)

**Adjectives come in handy when describing a noun. Adjectives describe a person , place or thing (object = vase).
Adjectives answer *what kind, which one, how man ?* A question will begin with the following words: what kind? which one? how many?**

see	_touch_	_hear_	_taste_	_smell_
fancy	hug	bark	sweet	stinky
tiny	grip	beep	bitter	rotten
large	soft	boom	sour	rancid
older	rough	shrill	salty	foul

- He was dripping _**wet**_ in his **clothes** from head to toe (adjective: wet, clothes = _noun_)
- The train had a _**shrill**_ **whistle**.
- _**Bitter**_ **lettuce** does not taste good.

Adverbs that Tell

An adverb will give information that gives detail on how something was done. Interrogation begins with each of the following words: where, when, how.

Adverbs that tell *Where*

above	down	inside	anywhere	everywhere
outside	here	there	backward	near
up				

Adverbs that Tell *When*

before	immediately	sometimes	daily
late	soon	periodically	lately
suddenly	eventually	never	then

finally	now	today	first
often	tomorrow	forever	seldom
tonight	frequently	yesterday	early

Adverbs that Tell *How*

quietly	quickly	easily	silently
carefully	happily	badly	slowly
sweetly	too	loudly	mercifully

Tone of a Character

A fictional story uses the tone of a character in many ways. The tone of a person's words and their attitude give inside information about the character. The major and minor characters' personality should be planned in advance of writing a novel. A minor character may be *jealous* and *envious* of the main character and thereby, will try to destroy the reputation of the main character.

- Some characters are optimistic, positive, bright, cheerful, confident, assertive, and self-reliant.
- Some characters may have hurt feelings: cold, dejected, miserable, unhappy gloomy, dismal.
- Compassionate: kind, considerate, caring, generous, charitable, respectful, thoughtful.
- Agitated: nervous, frantic, tense, stressed, anxious, up tight, edgy.

- Questioning: curious, probing, nosey, perplexed, inquisitive, inquiring
- Hopeful: positive, optimistic, expectant, encouraging, likely
- Nervous: worried, edgy, panicky, jumpy, tense, touchy, restless

A short story of fiction or non-fiction must have the ***rising action, climax,*** ***falling action***, and ***a resolution***. Much time is spent on giving details about the location of the story. A description of the character and the problem they will try to solve. The ***main character*** will try to ***solve the problem*** several times unsuccessfully. It gives the story suspense, and **it makes the story interesting to the reader.** In the end, the main character solves the problem.

~What does a novel need to keep the interest of the reader?~

A main character may struggle through an ***emotional problem***. A main character may have ***internal conflict*** because they may be afraid of heights, or riding in an elevator.

A ***minor character*** may be ***jealous*** or ***envious*** of the main character. An ***external conflict*** happens when the minor character tries to destroy the reputation of a major character.

Point of view refers to the narration of the story. The usage of pronouns lets the reader know the story is narrated from first person point of view by using words like: I, me, mine, we, and ours. If the story is narrated by third person, the key words are: he, him, she, her, and them.

If you look at young children's books, three verbs are used to describe action. For instance, the "ing" verb must have three consistent endings of words with "ing." Whatever, the verb endings, they must be the same. In addition, a verb ending in "s" requires additional verbs with an "s" ending.

running, jumping, skipping

In addition, the "ed" has three different sounds when it comes to endings. The first sound for "ed" ends in a "d" sound. Then the second "d" sounds like a "t" for an ending. And the last sound has and "e-d" sound for an ending. The writer must be consistent when using words ending in "ed."

"d" = would   "t" = kicked   "e-d" = twisted

Story #2
Title: *Stan Loves Chocolate*

Introduction 1st paragraph
(Snicker bar, chocolate ice cream, a chocolate donut)

Stan visited a factory that made pastry. He fell in love with chocolate examples to eat. He ate a *chocolate* ice cream **Snicker bar**, some *chocolate* **ice cream**, and a *chocolate* **donut.**

2ⁿᵈ paragraph
(First sentence in paragraph two introduces the topic of Snicker bars.)

Before Stan knew it, **he** ate a whole box of chocolate Snicker bars. "Wow, these bars are fantastic," said Stan. They are filled with peanuts and chocolate that gives you energy and a good snack to eat. I wonder what a Snickers bar would taste like, if it had white chocolate? **Subsequently, Stan** finished all his Snicker bar samples and was ready to enjoy and experience the samples of a chocolate ice cream stand that was located nearby.

3ʳᵈ paragraph
(verb included in sentence)
(Third paragraph introduces the topic of homemade chocolate ice cream.)

Without knowing it, **Stan** was standing in front of a lady who was making homemade chocolate ice cream. He patiently waited to get a scoop of her chocolate ice cream. **As** she gave samples of ice cream to eat, **customers** lined up to get a sample. Stan was given a chocolate ice cream treat on a waffle cone to enjoy.
After visiting two stations at the pastry show, **Stan** loved the smell of donuts.

4ᵗʰ paragraph
(verb included in sentence)
(Fourth paragraph introduces the topic of a chocolate donut.)

He followed a wonderful aroma that led him to a chocolate donut shop. There were many varieties of donuts, and Stan purchased a dozen chocolate donuts to take home. **In the meantime, Stan** sampled one of the chocolate donuts with chocolate nuts on top. The donut was delicious!

5th paragraph

Conclusion: Not given in this example.

Chocolate = *white* chocolate, *milk* chocolate, *dark* chocolate

****

Story #3
Title: *Horses*

Introduction 1st paragraph

After school, Carol learned her Dad had sold her horse. He was fearful the horse would fall down with Carol on it. The legs and each hoof on the horse had inflammation that could not be reversed. Carol's Dad gave her the option of buying a new horse to ride. **In the** newspaper, three **horses** were for sale: A Palomino, a Shetland Pony, and a Tennessee Walker.

2nd paragraph
(First sentence introduces the topic of the Palomino horse.)

With her parents help, **they** phoned the owner and asked if they could see the Palomino horse the owner had for sale. The hair on the palomino was a golden color with a white mane and tail. Carol's Dad opened the mouth of the Palomino to find the age of the horse. The horse was around two years of age and was green broke. **In other words,** **he** needed to be trained to have a saddle on his back and then a rider. Carol would have to train the horse to accept a saddle on his back; before she could ride him. Her Dad told the owner, Carol needed time to make a decision on which horse to buy.

3rd paragraph
(First sentence in paragraph three introduces the topic of the Shetland pony.)

By the roadside, **Carol** and her **Dad** stopped to see a Shetland pony. The pony had large red and white patches on the body. The Shetland pony had short legs. Carol noticed the mane and tail were whitish in color. They found the horse was smaller than Carol expected. A miniature pony would have a difficult time carrying Carol's long legs. **Consequently,** **they** let the owner know that Carol was not interested in the Shetland pony. **So,** **they** rushed to see the Tennessee Walking horse that was a mile away.

4th paragraph
(First sentence in paragraph four introduces the Tennessee Walking horse.)

In the next farm field, a tall black Tennessee Walking **horse** was grazing in the pasture. It was a beautiful black horse with a black mane and tail. Carol rode the Tennessee Walking horse and fell in love with the easy, comfortable ride the Tennessee Walker provided. She said it was like sitting in a big rocking chair at home. The ride was smooth with the Tennessee Walker taking long strides in walking because of his long legs.

5th paragraph

No Conclusion

There are no replacement words given in the Thesaurus Dictionary for the different horses. It is not always possible to replace words. To replace words, you must choose nouns that can be replaced in the introduction.

****

Story #4
Title: *Ducks*

Introduction 1st paragraph
(Mallard, American, Mandarin)

There are many different breeds of ducks that live on the earth. Some live in the wild and some ducks live on farms in North America. Webbed feet ducks are some like the **Mallard** *duck*, **American** *Coot*, and the *Mandarin duck* may have different colors, but they have one thing in common. They have webbed feet. Ducks are intelligent and love to snuggle up with a person because they are sociable creatures.

2nd paragraph
(First sentence in paragraph two introduces a sentence about Mallards.)

In *the early morning hours*, **you** will see a Mallard duck swimming in a pool of water. Mallards are dabbing ducks. In a foot of water or more, a *Mallard* will tip his or her beak into shallow water to get their food from plants beneath the surface of the water. They never dive. A Mallard has a short neck and he has several different colors on his body. They eat the stems and leaves of plants, small fish, and insects. Their webbed feet help a Mallard to swim in the water.

3rd paragraph
(First sentence in paragraph third introduces the topic sentence about the American Coot.)

In *all fairness*, the **American Coot** is plump and looks little like a chicken because he has a rounded head and his bill slopes. He is mostly a dark grayish black color. The American Coot has a white bill and a brown spot above his bill. They have short wings on their body. Coots have webbed feet for swimming. He bobs his head back and forth sticking his beak into the water for food. They do not dive in the water. The ducks lay eggs every day like the chickens, but they are not sold in stores. **In** *the summertime,* **they** like to swim in freshwater lakes. Coots get their nourishment from different grasses growing under the surface of the water. They eat pondweeds, sedges, grasses, algae, tadpoles, small fish, worms and snails. Both the Coot and Mandarin duck have a similar diet. In our quest for ducks, we saw another group of ducks.

4th paragraph
(First sentence in paragraph fourth introduces the Mandarin duck.)

Across the field, **we** spotted a Mandarin duck and he looked beautiful. He had many colors. **In** our research, **we** found they mostly live in Eastern China, Japan, Korea, and parts of Russia. They are migratory birds and can be found in California and Florida. Mandarin hatcheries raise and sell their Mandarin ducks to the public. They range from a hundred to six hundred dollars because they are rare birds. Mandarin ducks have webbed feet, and they like to bob their beak in the water to search for food beneath the surface of the water. They eat plants and leaves of plants below the surface of the water. A Mandarin diet is made up of seeds to eat, a plant, and some small fish.

5th paragraph

No Conclusion

****

Story #5
Title: *Chicken Eggs*
(Araucana, Cochin, Leghorn)

1st paragraph

Did you know there are ten different kinds of chickens? You will learn about three different chickens that lay eggs every day. Some eggs are sold in the store. Also, some chickens have beautiful colored feathers. The *Araucana chicken, Cochin chicken,* and a *Leghorn chicken* have different colored feathers. Some chickens are more striking in color than others.

2nd paragraph
(First sentence in paragraph two introduces the topic sentence about the Araucana chicken.)

Did you know the *Araucana* chicken has an aggressive personality? <u>At feeding *time*,</u> **they** will peck another chicken's behind. **Therefore**, **they** need to be watched. They have a lot of feathers on each side of the beak, and their feathers are bushy. They came from Chili to North America in the late 1920s and early 1930s. An Araucana chicken lays blue and greenish eggs and are not sold in stores. They have a red comb above their beak and a flabby comb of red skin that hangs below the beak. Araucana has a long neck, and he has an orange reddish color that is further down his neck. The lower part of his neck has some blondish looking feathers. The tips of his wings have an orange-red color. While the remainder of his body has dark colored feathers. **However**, our Cochin chicken has a different personality to what most farm families like to have on their farm.

3rd paragraph
(The third paragraph introduces a topic sentence about the Cochin chicken.)

  The *Cochin chicken* can live in a warm or cold climate because of the *large* feathers. Cochins' have a calm personality, and they get along with other chickens. **With the presents of gravel**, a **Cochin** will pick at the gravel because it helps them to digest their food by removing the dust particles on the pebble. They also dust themselves with the dirt, or dust from the pebble. Cochin chickens can be all white in color with a large comb on top of their head. They have a reddish and black feathers on their body. Furthermore, they can grow up to twelve pounds. The Cochin chicken immigrated from the Shanghai province of China in 1840. Consequently, another immigrant chicken arrived from Italy in 1828.

4th paragraph
(Fourth paragraph introduces the topic of the Leghorn chicken).

 In the beginning, the **Leghorn** chicken arrived from Italy. At first the Leghorn chicken was called the Italian chicken. **Through the years, they** slowly became known as the Leghorn chicken. They became the Leghorn chicken in 1865. They love to scratch for their food among the grass that grows in the field. Leghorn chickens have thick feathers so they can easily live with colder temperatures. The Leghorn comes in a variety of colors. Some are white, brown, black and buff in color. **For instance,** a **Leghorn chicken** will lay almost three hundred white eggs or more. They rarely fight. **In fact, they** make good house pets. The rooster may weigh around eight pounds while the hen weighs five pounds. They are economical because they like to eat grass and roam on pastureland where grasses grow.

5th paragraph

No Conclusion

 Instead of a name change, adjectives will be used to replace some of the words used to describe each one of the three chickens. In the summary, the chickens' names cannot be replaced with a noun. Describing the chicken with adjectives may be interesting in the summary to the reader.

Story #6
Title: *Dogs and Cats*
(compare and contrast writing)

1st paragraph (dogs)

Overall, a **dog** is submissive because they need to connect with the owner. Dogs are good companions for humans. A human and a dog will share a walk together. ***Also, as you know,*** **dogs** are territorial animals. Dogs are good hunters. **If** a dog licks the hand of his master with his tongue, **he** is showing admiration and submissiveness to his owner. A dog is easy to teach because they have been taught by their owner to go outside to potty. Dogs range in size from small dogs to larger dogs like the Saint Bernard. They live an average of seven years but some as much as twenty years. Dogs have emotional needs, and they relate to a human's emotional need.

2nd paragraph (cats)

As *i*n my aunt's case, her **cat** saved her life. **Upon** smelling the fumes in the kitchen, Hershey jumped up on my aunt's stomach and woke my aunt up. The fireman came and fixed the gas leak. The firemen said, "Cats are sociable creatures and they like humans." They are territorial by nature and warn other animals to stay away. **Also,** **cats** are carnivorous and love meat. They may sleep well beyond nine hours. **In** this way, **they** conserve energy. Cats are nocturnal animals. They have excellent hearing and vision. They will sit for a long time focusing on capturing a bird. Their tail helps to keep them balanced. **In addition**, a **cat** has sharp claws and teeth to help with hunting for food because they can strike with powerful claws and sharp teeth. A cat is an independent creature.

3rd paragraph (similarities)

Both dogs and cats share attributes of helping support a human emotionally. **Often, dogs** and **cats** can feel the stress of a human. **Thus,** a **dog** and a **cat** give comfort, and companionship when an adult needs it emotionally. Smaller dogs and larger dogs like to be petted. A small dog and a cat like to snuggle up close to a human being. **Furthermore, dogs** and **cats** come in a variety of sizes. Both animals have a body, perky ears, four legs and a tail. **Likewise,** a **dog**, may have a fluffy tail like some cats do. Dogs and cats have furry hair which keeps them warm in the wintertime. Both the dog and the cat are affectionate animals.

4th paragraph (contrast)

Furthermore, cats can easily jump up on a five - foot fence and sit or walk on the slim board on the opposite side of the fence. They may be looking to catch a butterfly or bird. **What's more,** a cat can effortlessly climb a tree. **However,** a **dog** does not climb trees or walk on top of a fence. Dogs may jump over a smaller fence, but they do not climb a fence.

****

Story #7
Title: *Oil*

Introduction 1st paragraph
(Three nouns that support oil. Oil produces: tires, boxes, vehicles).

Oil has many uses and helps to produce a variety of products. Oil is used to make many kinds of **tires**, different styles of **boxe**s to ship machinery, and a variety of **vehicles**. Every business runs on oil products. Fertilizer is made for farmers to grow feed for animals and human consumption of food products.

2nd paragraph (tires)

Oil helps to produce a *variety* of **tires** for skateboards, bicycles, and a variety of vehicles. Different cars use a larger or a smaller tire. Pickup trucks, tractors, semi-trucks, and caterpillars require different treads and a thicker tread to run smoothly on the job. Oil is needed to make good strong tires to last thousands of miles before another tire replaces the old tire. ***Without oil,* we** would all be walking to the store for goods and to work at our jobs. Progress happens when oil produces a rubber tire. Our bikes and cars ride smoother and more comfortably because they are made from oil. **Without tires**, there would be no **vehicles** such as: cars, buses, taxis, pickups, trucks, vans or large vehicles to haul our products. ***Instead,* we** would be carrying items to and from work. Oil makes the plastic bags that we use for groceries. Oil makes tires that provide transportation for people around the world. A wooden wheel does not provide a good ride.

3rd paragraph (boxes)

For instance, **oil** helps produce boxes to ship thousands of products. The conveyor belt helps to deliver many different kinds of products from one place to another in a short amount of time. A worker receives the material to work on and then sends it to another worker. As a result, a car, has many parts that connects to the automobile because it is made from oil. ***In fact, car parts*** are made in other states and countries. Boxes are used to ship parts and equipment from one factory to another factory. Oil makes our lives easier because it oils squeaky doors and keeps our cars running on the road. Oil produces boxes for jewelry, auto parts, heaters, and utensils for the kitchen. Almost every item shipped will come in a box that oil helped produce. Boxes make life easier for delivering goods. Even pizza comes in a box. **As we have seen, oil** is needed to keep modern conveniences. We are blessed as a nation to have oil and the men who drill for oil every day.

4th paragraph (vehicles)

Oil is a blessing because it produces many products besides vehicles. **For** example, **oil** is used to heat buildings and to produce electricity. **Furthermore,** oil makes products like plastic bags, polyurethane solvents, material for clothes, airplane parts, computers, cell phones, water pipes, shampoo, nylon, and guitar strings. Oil makes credit cards and a multitude of items not mentioned. Our lives have been enriched with oil. Oil isn't just for cars. **By** drilling for oil, **we** will make America; energy independent.

5th paragraph

No Conclusion

Oil = lubricant
Boxes = packages
Vehicles = automobiles

****

Story #8
Title: *Water*
Begin the first sentence with water. Find three nouns to support water. (Examples: cooking, swimming, bathing)

Introduction 1st paragraph

<u>*As an illustration*</u> **water** is a liquid, we cannot live without it. It serves many areas of our life. Water is used for **cooking**, **swimming**, and **bathing**. Our body is made up of seventy-five percent water.

2nd paragraph
(The second paragraph will be about *cooking* with water.)

In <u>fact,</u> **vegetables** *such as carrots* and *potatoes* need cleaning in water before placing them in a pot of water to cook on the stove. We use water to boil spaghetti, macaroni, rice, and to cook mashed potatoes to eat. **Likewise, in dry years, water** needs to be conserved so every household does not go without water for hygiene purposes.

3rd paragraph
(The third paragraph will begin with *water*.)

Admittedly, water gives a lot of pleasure. It is great for exercising and to relax in a pool of water after a hard day at work. A pool of water adds laughter and many people enjoy trying to float on top of the water. **In a desert climate, water** is appreciated. Some people do not water their lawns to conserve water. As mentioned earlier, **on** hot days, **relatives** and **friends** enjoy water and a pool party. **In** lean years, every drop of **water** is appreciated all year round. Water is essential in every aspect of our lives and is needed to keep good hygiene to keep healthy.

4th paragraph
(The fourth paragraph introduces bathing.)

On hot sweaty days, **bathing** is a wonderful way to clean up and feel refreshed. Bathing in a tub of water or taking the time to take a quick shower refreshes the body. Water is used to wash the hair and clean the scalp of dandruff. A hot, warm or cold-water shower helps sooth and relax painful muscles. Water is essential for a civilized society to flourish. Humans and animals need water to survive.

5th paragraph

No Conclusion

Cooking - cuisine, food
Swimming - drenched
Bathing - washing, soaking, cleaning

****

Story #9
Title: *Lights*

1st paragraph
(Find three adjectives to describe lights.)

Lights are important in our daily lives. We use **flashing-colored lights** to warn us about danger ahead. *<u>Traffic</u>* **lights are used** at a four way intersection, and a *<u>flash</u>* **light** is used when electrical power lines are down. Flashing red lights are associated with police cars, fire trucks, and an ambulance. Motorist must give the right of way to emergency vehicles.

2nd paragraph
(The second paragraph sentence begins with flashing-colored lights.)

Why are flashing red lights important? **<u>For example,</u>** red **lights** flashing help to warn drivers that the bridge may not safe to cross. What's more, red lights could warn drivers of a horrific accident that took place ahead of them. A red light is a caution light to warn drivers that an emergency vehicle is needed to control traffic. Red and blue lights are the symbol of a police presence. Police are present to save lives and to keep drivers safe. Fire fighters flash red and white colored lights in an emergency. While an ambulance driver will flash red and yellow lights in an emergency. Flashing red lights caution a driver to slow down and proceed with caution. Motorist may be required to stop to keep people safe and avoid having an accident.

3rd paragraph
(The third paragraph must begin with traffic lights. yellow - adjective.)

<u>**Without a doubt**</u>, traffic **lights** are necessary to keep motorists safe while driving. <u>**As** a precaution,</u> a yellow **light** cautions drivers to prepare to stop. <u>**However,**</u> if the **motorist** is traveling too fast to stop, they may keep driving while the yellow light is showing. **In** *short,* a red *light* means a motorist must stop. Pedestrians have the right to cross the street using the crosswalk. A traffic light at an intersection or a four-way stop is needed to help drivers know who has the right away in driving. <u>Afterall</u>, another good source of light to use in an emergency is the flashlight.

4th paragraph
(The fourth paragraph will begin the sentence about flashlights.)

In <u>an electrical storm,</u> a *flashlight* becomes necessary. A high intensity storm may knock out the electrical power grid for homes and businesses. **Therefore,** a **flashlight** helps a person to see in the dark. People who have glaucoma cannot see the shapes and cannot distinguish if the object is a piece of furniture or a person. A small light fixture will help a glaucoma person to see what they could not see in total darkness. **In** addition, a flashing **flashlight** is necessary in warning people on the roadway of danger and to use caution in driving. **With** a bridge out, **flashing-lights** are essential in keeping people safe.

<u>**5th paragraph**</u>

No Conclusion

Replace words with different words in the order that was listed in the introduction.

Flashing lights = blinking lights
Traffic light = stoplight
Flashlight= bright light, luminous light

****

Story #10
Title: *Soap*

1st paragraph (soap)
*Three kinds of adjectives that describe soap are used in the introduction. * (liquid soap, shampoo, detergent)

In the stores, **soap** is on the shelves. They have different soap products available that provide different needs. Stores offer a liquid soap, a **shampoo** soap for hair, and a **detergent** soap for washing clothes. Many companies make a variety of soap to help families at home or on the job. Soap comes in many flavors that help with hygiene and being clean.

2nd paragraph
(The second paragraph introduces the liquid soap. (liquid-adjective)

First, liquid **soap** comes in several different flavors. A liquid soap is for washing the hands. Some hand liquid soaps have a moisturizing factor to moisture dry hands. Other soaps are antibacterial soaps and are used in health facilities. A liquid soap may come in a foam. The foam makes it easier to wash hands or it may be used as a body soap while showering. A lot of vitamins help to create moisture in the soap with the smell of coconut soap or a vanilla flavored soap. **For** instance, **soap** keeps one feeling fresh and clean and smelling refreshed all day long. **Furthermore,** liquid **soap** is used to clean dishes and stubborn spots on a plate. Sometimes the stubborn spots need washing by hand and then placed in a dish washer to sanitize the plate. **Additionally**, a liquid **soap** helps to clean the dirty silverware, and it will make pots and pans sparkle like new.

3rd paragraph
(The third paragraph introduces shampoo in the first sentence.)

In a colorful bottle, a **shampoo** label will address fine hair, thick hair, or damaged hair. **For** instance, **shampoos** may add volume to hair which will boost the hair without removing moisture from the hair. **In** addition, some **shampoos** will help to keep tinted or colored hair from fading too soon. **Subsequently**, **shampoos** are made to thicken fine hair by using their shampoo. There are shampoos that are made for oily or greasy hair. Teasing hair too much may dry out the hair. The hair then needs a shampoo and conditioner that will relax the hair and give the hair a silkier and softer feel to the hair. **Also**, clean **hair** and clean **clothes** are refreshing and boosts the spirit of a person after a long day at work.

4th paragraph
(The fourth paragraph introduces detergent soap.)

A detergent is used for washing clothes, but manufacturers have their job cut out for them. **As a result, manufactures** make soap for acidic water. Hard Water requires a softener when washing clothes. **In washing clothes today**, a tablespoon of **detergent** will clean the clothes, and it will protect a washing machine from wearing out too soon. Knowing the type of water your house has will help you select a good detergent for laundering clothes. **Additionally,** some **detergents** have more bleach in their product than others. The bleach helps to whiten and clean-clothes.

5th paragraph

No Conclusion

Sequentially replace the word used in the introduction with a new synonym. Words need to be listed in the order as written in the introduction.

liquid = liquified
shampoo = clean hair
detergent = laundry agent

****

Story #11
Title: *Paper*
Three nouns have been selected for the product of paper: magazine, plates, labels

Introduction 1st paragraph

Paper products are used daily in writing articles for a **magazine**, making paper **plates**, and **labels** to send packages. Paper is smooth and is easy to write notes and reminders when appointments are scheduled.

2nd paragraph
(*Magazine bears the topic sentence for the paragraph.*)

Within a magazine, **they** have different articles to read. **On** *the shelves,* a **customer** can read the newspaper headlines about politics, what is happening in the community, a musical event or a sports event that will take place in a city or town. All of the events bring in revenue and business people look forward to helping their community. **Besides**, a **community** gathering needs delicious food and paper plates to bring people together to celebrate the fun occasion.

3rd paragraph (paper plates)

In *the store,* paper **plates** are on the shelves. There are thin paper plates, colorful *paper* plates, thicker *paper* plates. If you are having a party, you will want to purchase a plate that is functionable for the event. Some meat and cooked foods are heavier than other food products. **Therefore**, heavier paper **plates** are needed to hold the food. Big outdoor events need *paper* plates and napkins to make the outing successful with good food to eat. **In the meantime**, paper **plates** make an event more enjoyable. A picnic near a lake is a good place to have paper plates to eat food. *In* the morning, a paper **bowl** can hold a variety of fruit. Water or a soda in a paper cup is awesome. **Equally important**, are **labels** that help us identify a vegetable or fruit product in a can.

4th paragraph
(The first sentence is about labels)

  Without labels on canned goods, *we* as a customer would have to open the can to see what vegetable or fruit would be inside the can. **Subsequently**, young **companies** use labels on their vitamin bottles. People like to read labels on a package before they purchase the product. **Likewise,** the **pharmacy** uses labels to place the dosage, the name of the person, and the doctors name on the prescription medicine bottle. Advertisement labels are placed in mailboxes that use paper products. The United States Post Office uses labels to address packages that are sent rapidly through the mail. Labels and paper products are needed to keep order and to avoid confusion.

5th paragraph

No Conclusion

Magazine = periodical, publication
Plate = dish
Labels = sticker

****

Story #12
Title: *Mark the Shark (Story)*
(A story written from the shark's point of view).

1st paragraph
(description, habitat, diet)

My name is Mark, and I am a Great White Shark. Would you like a **description** of me, my **habitat,** and about my **diet**?

2nd paragraph

M*y body top is grayish blue in color or it may be a grayish brown*. I am white underneath and the tips of my fins are black. **Thus, I** have a sleek physical body and as an adult my length is six meters, or twenty feet. I weigh 1,900 kilograms. **Consequently, my** size varies and my color can fool some of the sea animals. **Beside** a rock, I look like an old rock under the surface of the sea.

3rd paragraph
(adverbs tell where)

Frequently, I search for food while I am diving and swimming and doing flip flops in the Pacific and Atlantic Ocean. **Underneath the ocean surface, plants** and *hills* dominate the bottom of the ocean floor. Sometimes, there are schools-of- fish to eat because they swim together.

4th paragraph

In the meantime, I am always hunting for food to eat. <u>Without a doubt,</u> **my** prey are fish, sharks, sea animals, seals, rays, tuna, dolphins, and porpoises. They make a delicious meal. My favorite prey are seals and sea lions because they are soft and moist. Some of my prey get away, but sea animals make a good meal for breakfast.

5th paragraph

Description = picture
Habitat = ocean, Pacific Ocean, Atlantic Ocean
Diet = food

Now, you have a *picture* of me in words and that I come in different colors and sizes. My home is in the *ocean* and you know the *food* I like to eat. I hope to see you. You are welcome to come and swim with me in the Pacific or Atlantic Ocean.

Story #13
(Single paragraph illustrating prepositional phrases and transition words)

Do you know who built the first car? In 1885, Carl Benz invented the first gasoline engine car and he applied for a patent in 1886. **Equally important,** the **electric cars** were produced in 1888.

Electric trains were built too. **However,** Ford started a new company building gasoline cars. His partnership dissolved and Cadillac and Buick began making cars that competed against the Ford and the Mercedes Benz company. The electric car was flourishing in 1912 until 1929. **But**, **Ford** wanted to make cars affordable for the customer to buy his cars. Thomas Robbin**,** invented a conveyor belt and Ford used it in 1929. To deliver car parts to the next worker to assemble. Subsequently, the electric car sold for $1,750 dollars, but the gasoline car that Ford built sold for $650 dollars.

****

Story #14
Title: *Money*
(one paragraph)

    For *instance,* ***money*** comes in different denominations. Coins range from one cent to fifty cents. **Whereas** the paper dollar begins with a denomination of a one-dollar bill and will range up to one thousand dollars. Rarely do we see a thousand-dollar bill. **Consequently**, paper ***money*** has denominations in fives, tens, twenties, and hundred-dollar bills. **However,** the best **money** is a silver coin, a silver dollar, or silver bar. Gold has a higher value because it may be used in coins, jewelry, and in a small or larger gold bar. Equally important, gold is used to conduct electricity. Gold is made into a malleable wire, so electricity is generated in a home or business. **Currently,** a four-hundred-ounce large gold bar is worth a million dollars.

****

Story #15
Title: *Transparent Oil Products*

Oil and natural gas make MRI machines that saves lives, plus pacemakers, and defibrillators for the heart. Surgeons use many machines made from oil and natural gas to help humans. Hospitals, ambulances, fire trucks, and police cars have products that save lives. We have 132 oil and natural gas refineries in the USA. Our refineries are important because they evaluate the oil and natural gas to prepare and send it to the appropriate manufacturing businesses around the world. And to help reduce emissions for companies. **Consequently, we** are fortunate to have petroleum to make our lives better.

The 6,000 oil and natural gas products make prescription medicine and over the counter medicines. We have a variety of different materials that oil and natural gas provide. It produces electricity which heats our homes and provides light to see in the dark. A shower that gives a refreshing shower and a flushing toilet. Shampoos for the hair and different soaps to use at home. **In addition,**

oil and **natural gas** help to produce cement, asphalt, and steel that is used on the highway and to cross massive waterways around the world. **Moreover,** it provides the modern conveniences of a telephone, computer and television set. Oil and natural gas make 6,000 different products. They even make materials that produce clothes we wear.

****

Story #16
Title: *Lumpfish*
(Personification)

Do you know anything about me? Well, let me fill you in on who I am. I am considered to be a small fish and I live in the cold-water. I have a big blue puffy body and large pectoral fins that help me swim. My huge eyes help me to see some of my enemies who would like to eat me for breakfast, lunch or dinner. Because of the shape and the large fan like fins, I do not swim fast. **Besides, I** swim slow in the ocean. You can see me swimming in the Artic Ocean, North Atlantic, and the Pacific Ocean. Most of my friends who are small fish, swim faster than me. I have to look out for my adversaries who love to eat me. My adversaries are crabs, snails, tuna fish, sea anemones, and sharks. They live in ocean with me.

Do you know what my favorite food to eat in the ocean is? I love to eat plankton which is a plant that lives on the ocean floor. It grows near the shore and it lives in acidic water. You may find me at night among the eelgrass beds or around an area with kelp and where algae grows. **Oh, I** heard you want to know if I have teeth. **Instead, I** have needle sharp teeth with a lining that covers the rim of my bulbous lips.

Nevertheless, once a year, I look the male fish over to see who is the most handsome fish to mate with in the shallow part of the ocean. Most people would call our mating complex. **To me, I** think it is rather simple. Once a mate has been selected, and we have courted awhile, he leaves the deeper part of the ocean. He swims closer to the coastline to make a nest for me on the ocean floor or in the crevice of a solid area of a rock. I will lay the eggs and he will fertilize them after they have been laid. Around March or spring time, my mouth opens wide and out come the eggs. The eggs have a sticky spongy mucus that covers the eggs. **At first, my** eggs are pink when they have been laid. **However**, the **eggs** will soon change to green or yellow in color, and as time passes the color deepens. My eggs sink in the sandy water to the bottom. It takes four months to lay two batches of eggs. Once the eggs are laid, I swim away and my husband spends his time guarding my eggs until they hatch. **In fact, he** fans the eggs with his fin like fans. I lay from 140,000 up to 300,000 eggs twice in the spring time of the year.

People love to catch me in Europe to eat me and to make caviar using my eggs. They tell me my caviar tastes salty, bitter, and slightly salty. **If made right**, **my** caviar could pass for Black Caviar which is made in America and comes from my cousin, the sturgeon. It takes briny, nutty, and sweet. People love to eat my meat. People are predator like the advisories that I told you about earlier. **Well**, **I** hope you enjoy a good swim. **About** eight months out of a year, **I** swim in the deepest part of the ocean. You will see schools of fish swimming together in large groups of a hundred or more. Be careful as you swim, not to get caught by the humans when you move in closer to the shore line.

******

Story #17
Title: *Sarah's Trouble*

Rising Action

Sarah attended a ballet show. She was well dressed in her black dress, diamond necklace, and diamond earrings. Her wedding ring added to the glamor that evening. She caught the attention of everyone. After the ballet performance, a brief meeting was held on future ballets, orchestral, and stage performances being performed for the following year at the Civic Center. Sarah wanted to leave because she felt it might snow and she wanted to be home. She was glad she wore her white fur coat. She felt she would be safe walking to her car.

Her stiletto high heels clicked away as she left the ballet. Her car was not far away. It was parked near and alley way. As she walked in her high heels; she heard other foot steps behind her. Every hair on her body stood up and she desperately wanted to run, but she decided to quicken her pace. Sure enough, the stranger picked up the quickness of the steps.

Climax Mixed with Tension and Excitement

All of a sudden, Sarah felt her mouth covered with a gloved hand. Sarah was being dragged at knife point to a stranger's car. Sarah wondered if she was going to survive the evening. She felt the knife near her throat. What did the stranger want? Did he want to kidnap her? Did he want to kill her? Sarah didn't think about it any longer. She raised her stiletto high heels and stomped as hard as she could on the foot of her assailant. Sarah reached inside her coat pocket and pulled out some pepper spray. She turned spraying the stranger in the face. He was not capable of seeing. Sarah ran to her car that was parked near the alleyway.

Falling Action the Tension and Excitement Reduces

Upon arriving at her car, she called police who were nearby. A patrol car arrived in time to nab the stranger. The culprit had dropped his car keys when Sarah sprayed him with the pepper spray. He fumbled with trying to find his keys and was about to start his automobile when the police arrived. The police handcuffed the kidnapper. The outlaw confessed that he needed the money for a gambling debt.

Resolution Secrets are Revealed

The police took the assailant to the police headquarters. He was finger printed and was given a number to hold while a picture was taken of him. Derek, the thief wanted to sell the diamonds to pay for his gambling debt. Instead, Derek would spend five years in jail for attempted kidnapping and robbery.

****

There are four areas of writing to be familiar with in writing.

Expository – cause and effect, problems and solutions, compare and contrast.

Narrative – comparative – similarities and differences, autobiography, fairy tale, novel.

Descriptive Writing – Writing about oneself, poems, traveling, memory, experience writing about nature.

Persuasive Writing- ethos (ethical appeal), pathos- (emotional appeal) logos (logical appeal).

Some of the writings to examine for prepositional phrases and transitional phrase are listed.

autobiography	biography	directions
invitations	letters	Newspapers
poems	reports	fantasy stories
family – travel	fiction stories	non-fiction
humorous	mystery	romance
thriller		

Different Structures of Writing

cause and effect   sequence and chronological order

compare and contrast   statements and conclusions

conflict and resolution   description

main idea and detail   problem and resolution

theme, essay, academic topic   news article

mystery.

Summary

    As promised, I have tried to share with you secrets about punctuation and where it is placed in a sentence. It is my hope, you will study the mini- lessons and examples on punctuation marks and where to place them in a sentence. Prepositions and transitive words give life to a document or story by connecting ideas for the reader. Nouns, pronouns, verbs, adjectives, and adverbs help with pinning down the details and the point of the writing. They also can help build suspense in a novel. It is my desire to see you have fun with writing now and in the future. Moreover, I wish the best for the purchaser of Rocket Writing to be successful and confident in writing and punctuating.

Bibliography

- John E. Warner and Francis Griffith <u>English Grammar and Composition</u> Harcourt, Brace & World, Inc. New York 1957.

- Susan Thurman, <u>The Only Grammar Book You Will Ever Need,</u> Adams Media Avon, Massachusetts, 2003

- Marvin Terban, <u>Checking your Grammar and Getting it Right</u> Scholastic Inc., 1993.

- L. Sue Baugh, <u>Essentials of English Grammar</u> A Practical Guide to the Mastery of English, Passport Books, Lincolnwood, Illinois, 1995.

- Robert Britain, <u>A Pocket Guide to Correct Punctuation,</u> Barron's Educational Series, Inc., Woodbury, New York, 1981.

- Edward Fry, Ph.D. and Elizabeth Sakley, Ed.D. <u>Dr. Fry's Beginning Writers Manual Spelling Checker, Grammar Rules and Suggested</u> Topics, Teachers Created Materials, Inc, Westminster, CA 92683, 2000.

- California State Text-Book Committee, W.W. Shannon, Superintendent,

- <u>English Lessons Book Two.</u> California State Series, 1903.

- Raquel Jaramillo, <u>The Complete Middle School Study Guide Everything You Need to ACE English Language Arts in One Big Fat Notebook</u>. work, Workman Publishing Company, Inc., 2019.

- Martyn J. Walsh and Anna Kathleen Walsh<u>, Plain English Handbook,</u> McCormick Mathers Publishing Company, Inc. Wichita, Kanas 1959.

- Thesaurus Vocabulary, Microsoft, 2024.
  http://grammar.ccc.comment.edu/grammar/transitions.hym 2024

www.ingramcontent.com/pod-product-compliance
Lightning Source LLC
Chambersburg PA
CBHW061821290426

44110CB00027B/2943